Bead by Bead

The Sorrowful Mysteries of the Rosary

By Stephanie Engelman

Cover art by Caris Roller
Graphic Design by Molly Evans, M. Evans Design

Printed in the United States of America

First Printing, 2020
ISBN 978-1-7345670-0-7

www.StephanieEngelman.com

Dedicated to my nephew, Jackson,
on the day of his First Holy Eucharist.

*May the life of Christ and his Holy Eucharist
always be your greatest source
of love, joy, and fulfillment.*

"If you wish peace to reign in your homes,
recite the family Rosary."

- *Pope Saint Pius X*

Introduction

The Rosary is such an important and beautiful prayer! Yet, when I prayed it with my young children, I found them squirming, complaining, and most definitely not meditating on the Biblical stories of each mystery! In an effort to alleviate this problem, I began to intersperse snippets of the Biblical stories between the Hail Mary's as we prayed.

This brought wonderful results with my own family, and I felt called to put it in writing. The printed format enabled me to address another difficulty I frequently encountered: the interminable question, "Mommy, what bead are we on?" Oh, how I wanted to immerse myself in prayer with my children, but that question was a constant distraction!

To solve this challenge, I added color coding to the Hail Mary's of the book, and made sets of sacrifice beads with each of my children that matched the pattern of Hail Mary beads in the book. Thus, as I pointed to each Hail Mary, my children could easily see the answer to their question!

If you'd like to make similar sacrifice beads or a pony bead rosary with your own children, you can find instructions on my website: www.StephanieEngelman.com/bead-by-bead.

I pray that this book (and the other books in the *Bead by Bead* series) will enrich your family's prayer of the Rosary. May you have peace in your homes and in your hearts!

In Christ,

Stephanie Engelman

A Note for Children

The Rosary is the Blessed Mother Mary's very special prayer. She gave it to us so that we could know and love her Son, Jesus, better.

When we pray the Rosary, we ask the Blessed Mother, Mary, to guide us on a beautiful journey. She walks with us through her Son's life and helps us to know and love him better.

Countless miracles have happened through the Rosary. Wars have been won, people who were very sick have been healed, and – most importantly – many, many people have been brought to Christ and his Church.

When you pray the Rosary, you can ask Mary to pray with you for things that are important to you. Do you know someone who's sick, or going through a difficult time? Is there something you're afraid of or worried about? Would you like to ask Jesus to help you to always love him? Or maybe you'd like to ask Jesus to help your priest, the leaders of your country, or your school?

While not every prayer is answered in the way we expect, offering our needs to God will always help us grow closer to Jesus. Plus, prayer gives us peace and joy, knowing that we are beloved children of God, and he has great plans for us!

Today, we will pray the Sorrowful Mysteries of the Rosary. They help us to think about how Jesus suffered and died for us. We usually pray these mysteries on Tuesdays and Fridays, or every day during Lent.

The Sorrowful Mysteries of the Rosary

Today, we offer our prayers for…

IN THE NAME OF THE FATHER
and of the Son, and of the Holy Spirit. Amen.

✚ I BELIEVE

in God, the Father Almighty, Creator of heaven and earth.
And in Jesus Christ His only Son, Our Lord,
Who was conceived by the Holy Spirit,
Born of the Virgin Mary,
Suffered under Pontius Pilate,
Was crucified, died and was buried.
On the third day, he rose again.
He ascended into Heaven,
and is seated at the right hand of God, the Father Almighty.
He will come again to judge the living and the dead.
I believe in the Holy Spirit,
the Holy Catholic Church,
the Communion of Saints,
the forgiveness of sins,
the resurrection of the body,
and life everlasting.
Amen.

OUR FATHER

who art in heaven, hallowed be thy name;
Thy kingdom come; thy will be done on earth, as it is in heaven.
Give us this day our daily bread;
and forgive us our trespasses,
as we forgive those who trespass against us;
and lead us not into temptation,
but deliver us from evil.
Amen.

HAIL MARY

full of grace, the Lord is with thee.
Blessed art thou among women,
and blessed is the fruit of thy womb, Jesus.
Holy Mary, Mother of God,
pray for us sinners now
and at the hour of our death.

HAIL MARY...

HAIL MARY...

GLORY BE

to the Father and to the Son and to the Holy Spirit. As it was in the
beginning, is now, and ever shall be, world without end. Amen.

OH MY JESUS,

forgive us our sins, save us from the fires of hell, and lead all souls
to heaven, especially those in most need of thy mercy.

The Agony in the Garden

As we meditate on the first Sorrowful Mystery of the Rosary, *The Agony in the Garden*, we see Jesus praying to God, his Father, just before he was arrested.

OUR FATHER...

🟡 HAIL MARY...

After sharing the Passover Meal with his Disciples, Jesus went to the Mount of Olives to pray.

🟤 HAIL MARY...

Jesus knew that he would be arrested that night, and that he would suffer and die on the cross the next day.

🟣 HAIL MARY...

He told the disciples that he was very sad, and asked them to wait, to keep watch, and to pray.

⚪ HAIL MARY...

Jesus walked away from the disciples and fell to his knees and prayed. He told God, his Father, that even though he didn't want to suffer and die on the cross, if it was what God wanted, he would do it.

● HAIL MARY…

Jesus went back to the disciples, but they had fallen asleep. He woke them and, once again, told them to pray.

● HAIL MARY…

Jesus returned to his place alone. He prayed so hard that he began to sweat, and the sweat turned to blood.

● HAIL MARY…

An angel of the Lord appeared to Jesus to ease his suffering.

● HAIL MARY…

Jesus returned to his disciples two more times, and found them sleeping each time.

● HAIL MARY…

After Jesus woke his disciples for the third time, soldiers came with a crowd of people, looking for Jesus.

● HAIL MARY…

Judas, the disciple who had turned against Jesus, walked up to him and gave him a kiss. The soldiers knew that this was Jesus, and they arrested him.

GLORY BE…

OH MY JESUS…

The Scourging at the Pillar

In the second Sorrowful Mystery, *The Scourging at the Pillar,* we watch as Jesus is sentenced to death and whipped and beaten.

OUR FATHER...

HAIL MARY...

When he was arrested, the soldiers took Jesus to the Jewish leaders, called the Sanhedrin.

HAIL MARY...

Jesus had spoken out against these leaders because they were very worried about following a long list of rules, but were forgetting to love God and their neighbors.

HAIL MARY...

The religious leaders of the Sanhedrin were angry with Jesus for speaking against them, and afraid that they would lose their power when more and more people followed Jesus.

HAIL MARY...

The leaders questioned Jesus. They were determined to find *something* that Jesus had done to break the law.

🔵 HAIL MARY…

The Sanhedrin found Jesus guilty of claiming to be the Son of God. They sent him to Pontius Pilate, the governor of Jerusalem, so that he could be sentenced to death.

🟢 HAIL MARY…

Pontius Pilate believed that Jesus was innocent. But the people yelled, "Crucify him!" and Pilate gave them what they wanted. He sentenced him to be scourged and crucified.

⚫ HAIL MARY…

The soldiers ripped Jesus' robe from his back and tied his hands.

🔴 HAIL MARY…

One of the soldiers whipped Jesus over and over again, while the crowd watched and cheered.

🔵 HAIL MARY…

Jesus didn't say a word, but endured all of this for you and for me.

🟣 HAIL MARY…

When you are sad or hurting, remember how sad and hurt Jesus must have been. Pray to him, and he will help you.

GLORY BE…

OH MY JESUS…

The Crowning with Thorns

As we pray the third Sorrowful Mystery, *The Crowning with Thorns,* we see the soldiers make fun of Jesus by placing a thorny crown on his head.

OUR FATHER...

🟡 HAIL MARY...

After the scourging, Jesus was exhausted. He had been awake all night long, with no sleep at all.

🟤 HAIL MARY...

His back, arms, and legs ached where the whip had cut him again and again.

🟣 HAIL MARY...

Sadly, Jesus' journey to the cross was nowhere near its end.

⚪ HAIL MARY...

The Roman soldiers wanted to make fun of Jesus.

🔵 HAIL MARY...

Once again, they tore the robe from his back. They dressed him in a soldier's red military cloak, to make him look like an earthly king.

HAIL MARY…

One of the soldiers wove together a crown of thorns.

HAIL MARY…

They pressed the crown onto Jesus' head. The thorns dug sharply into his skin.

HAIL MARY…

The soldiers brought Jesus out in front the crowd, hit him with a stick, and spit at him. They made fun of Jesus, saying, "Hail, King of the Jews!"

HAIL MARY…

The soldiers and the people watching didn't realize that Jesus was greater than any king they could imagine. He was – and is! – the King of heaven and earth.

HAIL MARY…

Jesus could have stopped them at any moment. But he chose to let these things happen, so that our sins can be forgiven, and we can live forever with him in heaven.

GLORY BE…

OH MY JESUS…

Carrying the Cross

Let us now walk with Mary as *Jesus Carries his Cross,*
the fourth Sorrowful Mystery of the Rosary.

OUR FATHER...

🟡 HAIL MARY...

After they had mocked him, the soldiers made Jesus pick up a
heavy wooden cross and begin the long walk to Calvary, where
he would be crucified.

🟤 HAIL MARY...

Tired, hungry, bruised and battered, the weight of the cross was
more than he could bear. Jesus stumbled and fell to his knees.

🟣 HAIL MARY...

Rising again to carry the cross, Jesus looked into the crowd and
saw his mother, Mary.

⚪ HAIL MARY...

Mary's heart ached as she looked into her son's eyes, and tears
streamed down her face.

🔵 HAIL MARY...

When the soldiers saw Jesus struggling to carry his cross, they
grew impatient. They took a man named Simon of Cyrene, and
forced him to carry the cross.

🟢 HAIL MARY…

A woman named Veronica stood watching. She wanted to do *something* to help Jesus. She gently wiped his face with a cloth.

⚫ HAIL MARY…

Jesus fell a second time, rocks digging into his hands as he hit the ground. But his long walk was not yet over. Slowly, he rose and continued the journey.

🔴 HAIL MARY…

Jesus also met the women of Jerusalem, who were crying. He told them not to cry for him, but to cry for themselves and their children.

🔵 HAIL MARY…

Jesus fell a third time. From where he lay, he could see Golgotha, the small hill on which he would be crucified.

🟣 HAIL MARY…

Slowly and painfully, Jesus walked up the hill. Finally, he arrived at his destination – the place where he would redeem the world.

GLORY BE…

OH MY JESUS…

The Crucifixion

In the final Sorrowful Mystery, we share in Mary's sadness as we remember *The Crucifixion of Jesus*.

OUR FATHER…

HAIL MARY…

The soldiers hung Jesus on the cross, while people nearby made fun of him. Jesus called out, "Father, forgive them, for they do not know what they are doing!"

HAIL MARY…

Two criminals were also crucified, one on each side of Jesus. One of them joined the crowd in teasing Jesus.

HAIL MARY…

The other criminal stopped the man, saying, "We have done something wrong, but this man has not." Then he said, "Jesus, remember me when you come into your kingdom."

HAIL MARY…

Jesus replied, "Amen, I say to you, today you will be with me in Paradise."

HAIL MARY…

Jesus saw his mother, Mary, standing with his beloved disciple, John.

🟢 HAIL MARY...

He said to Mary, "Woman, behold, your son." Then he said to John, "Behold, your mother." With these words, Jesus gave Mary to all of us as our Heavenly Mother.

⚫ HAIL MARY...

After several hours on the cross, Jesus cried out, "Father, into your hands I commend my spirit!" and he took his last breath.

🔴 HAIL MARY...

Darkness fell over the land, and the earth shook. The Roman soldiers became frightened. One of them said, "This man truly was the Son of God!"

🔵 HAIL MARY...

Jesus' body was placed in a tomb, and a heavy stone was rolled in front of the entrance.

🟣 HAIL MARY...

The story of Christ's crucifixion makes us very, very sad. However, we must remember that Jesus chose to die so that our sins could be forgiven. Three days later, he would rise again!

GLORY BE...

OH MY JESUS...

HAIL, HOLY QUEEN, MOTHER OF MERCY!

Hail, our life, our sweetness and our hope!
To thee do we cry, poor banished children of Eve.
To thee do we send up our sighs,
mourning and weeping in this valley of tears.
Turn then, most gracious advocate, thine eyes of mercy towards us
and after this, our exile, show unto us the
blessed fruit of thy womb, Jesus.
O clement, O loving, O sweet Virgin Mary!
Pray for us, O holy Mother of God,
That we may be made worthy of the promises of Christ.

OH GOD,

whose only-begotten Son,
by his life, death, and resurrection,
has purchased for us the rewards of eternal life,
grant, we beseech thee,
that by meditating on these mysteries
of the most holy Rosary of the Blessed Virgin Mary,
we may imitate what they contain
and obtain what they promise,
through the same Christ our Lord.
Amen.

IN THE NAME OF THE FATHER,

and of the Son, and of the Holy Spirit.
Amen.

Without the help of several faith-filled and generous Catholic women, this book might never have come to fruition.

Thank you, Laura Capes, for the (dare I say?) Spirit-inspired genius of the *Bead by Bead* title and for your editing prowess.

Thank you, Caris Roller, for the beautiful cover art. It's everything I had hoped it would be – and more.

Thank you, Molly Evans, for generously contributing your graphic design talents.

Thank you, MAMAS, for the support of your prayers – both for this book, and for my family.

Finally, thank you to the Blessed Mother. The list is too long. Just... *Thank You.*

Image Credits

- Cover: *Focus,* commissioned work by Caris Roller, 2019
- Page 3: Madonna with the Rosary, Bartolomé Esteban Murillo, 1650
- Page 5: The Madonna of the Rosary, Bartolomé Esteban Murillo, between circa 1675 and circa 1680
- Page 7: *Our Lady of the Rosary,* Michelangelo Merisi, between 1605
- and 1607
- Page 9: *The Agony in the Garden*, Andrea Mantegna, between 1458 and 1460
- Page 11: *An Angel Comforting Jesus Before His Arrest in the Garden of Gethsemane,* Carl Bloch, 1873
- Page 13: *Jesus in the House of Annas,* José de Madraza y Agudo, 1803
- Page 15: *Flagellation of Christ,* William-Adolph Bouguereau, 1880
- Page 17: *Christ Mocked,* Hieronymus Bosch, between 1479 and 1516
- Page 19: *Christ Mocked,* Pietro Della Veccia, C. 1650
- Page 21: *Christ Meets His Mother,* Gebhard Fugel, 1921
- Page 23: *Christ Falling on the Way to Calvary,* Raphael, c. 1516
- Page 25: *Christ at the Cross,* Carl Bock, c. 1870
- Page 27: *Descent from the Cross,* Peter Paul Rubens, c. 1613
- Page 29: *Harrowing of Hell*, Nikolay Koshelev, 1900

Except the cover, all images were sourced through Wikipedia and are public domain due to their publication prior to 1924.

About the Author

Stephanie Engelman is a wife and mother of five who lives in Indianapolis, Indiana. She is a convert to Catholicism and came to love the Rosary after it brought great peace during tumultuous times.

A public speaker who shares her personal experiences of Christ's peace and God's Providence, Stephanie is also the owner of Inkwell Personal Histories, through which she is blessed to learn and write about the lives of "everyday" men and women, creating books that become treasures for families and loved ones.

Stephanie is the author of the award-winning Catholic young adult novel, *A Single Bead*, a story about the power of prayer. She loves to pray her Rosary while walking in the evenings or hiking during the day, and also enjoys mountain biking, gardening, and snuggling her family.

Follow Stephanie on Facebook (@s.engelman.author) or Instagram (@stephanie_engelman). Her website is www.StephanieEngelman.com